Tangerine Press

an imprint of

SCHOLASTIC

www.scholastic.com

Scholastic and Tangerine Press and associated logos are trademarks of Scholastic Inc.

Published by Tangerine Press, an imprint of Scholastic Inc., 557 Broadway; New York, NY 10012

Scholastic Canada
Markham, Ontario

Scholastic Australia
Gosford, NSW

Scholastic New Zealand
Greenmount, Auckland

Scholastic UK
Warwickshire, Coventry

10 9 8 7 6 5 4 3 2 1

ISBN 0-439-87579-X

Printed and bound in China

CONTENTS

• HOW TO DRAW RAINFOREST ANIMALS

INTRODUCTION

It's a jungle out there! We're talking about the South and Central American rainforest—an amazing landscape full of equally amazing flowers, birds, trees, and animals. The Amazonian rainforest contains millions of acres of fascinating birds, mammals, reptiles, flowers, and trees.

In this book, you'll learn how to draw some of the wildlife that makes up this unique environment. Drawing requires a lot of patience and practice, so stick to it! You'll get better and better with each try. With the HB pencil in your kit, you can draw to your heart's content. Then, use the six colored pencils to add a little pizzazz to your drawing. The book will also give you some cool techniques and tricks to help you with your pictures. With all this help, you can create a beautifully colored rainforest of your own.

So, grab some paper and sharpen your pencils—you're about to draw some of the most interesting animals in the world!

MATERIALS

One of the nice things about drawing is that you need just a few basic supplies, like the ones in your kit. Before you begin, be sure you have all your materials handy so that you don't have to stop work to look for, say, an eraser.

1. Paper

Grab a stack of blank white sheets of paper in the size of your choice. Choose paper that isn't glossy or textured. Professional drawing paper works great if you don't mind the expense.

2. Pencils

You can pick up a set of good quality drawing pencils, including HB, 2B, 4B, and 6B. An HB pencil comes with this kit. The lighter HB and 2B pencils work best for basic drawing and for the finishing touches. The softer pencils, like the 4B and 6B, are used to add shading. Create a number of shades with just one pencil (like the HB) by decreasing or increasing the pressure.

3. Eraser

Keep a white eraser with sharp edges handy. Use the eraser not only to fix mistakes, but also to add highlights and textures.

4. Sharpener

Any type will do. You always want to have sharp points on your pencils for the cleanest drawings.

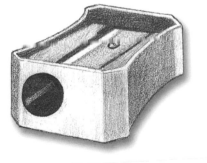

DRAWING TECHNIQUES

One of the most important things when it comes to drawing is to be comfortable with your materials.

1. First, try out the different pencils. Study the different strokes, line thicknesses, and how dark you can draw with your pencils.

2. Choose a soft pencil like a 2B, 4B, or 6B and try drawing straight parallel lines—vertical, diagonal, reverse, and horizontal. Practice this across a couple of pages, letting your hand move freely. This exercise may look too easy, but don't skip it because it will help you get comfortable with drawing pencils.

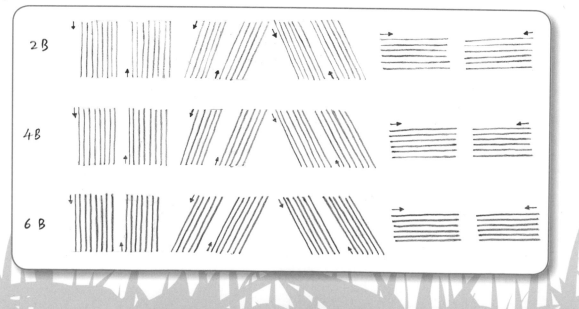

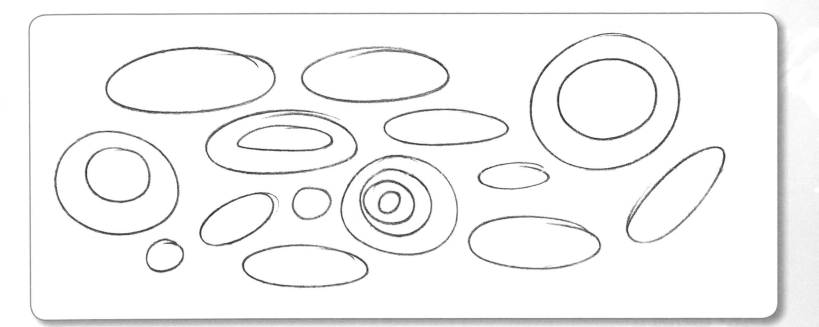

3. Practice drawing ovals and circles of various sizes. Use a 6B for this exercise. Draw the shape in one stroke, and draw it quickly. Use both sides of the paper and continue practicing for a while before starting to draw. Using quick, single strokes gives you a good judgment of form and volume, and makes your drawing more confident.

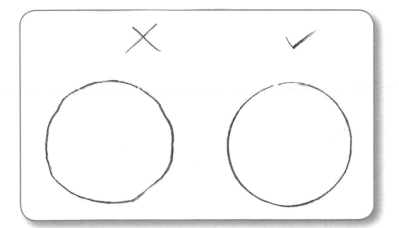

SHADING AND HIGHLIGHTING

1. Before you start shading, decide on the source of light. Shade the portions on the opposite side of the light, keeping in mind the volume of the drawing. If the shade portion is not rendered according to the surface or bulge of the animal, the drawing will look flat.

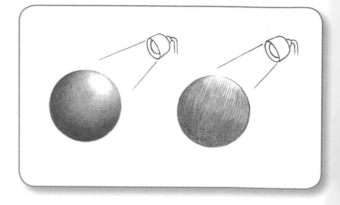

2. Shade doesn't necessarily mean black. It simply means less light. Try this exercise with all grades of pencils. Start shading horizontally or vertically, first using light pressure and then a heavier force. This will help you see the various tones you can achieve with the different pencils, which allows you to control your pencil according to the requirement.

3. You can add dark lines for the deepest folds or ground shadows once all the shading is done. This will enhance your drawing and make it look more three-dimensional.

4. A highlight is the brightest part of an object, where there is maximum light. It should be drawn in the direction of the light source. The highlighted area is to be left white, while the rest of the image is shaded. Highlights, especially of the eyes, add life to the image. If you forget to leave the highlight, just use the edge of your eraser to erase in the highlight!

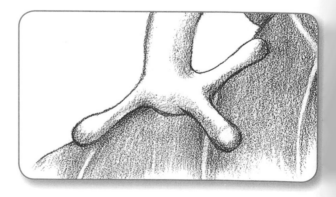

TEXTURES

Every surface has a texture—smooth, scaly, rough, or hard. Animals have textures, too (furry, scaly, feathery, or hairy). Practice shading by holding a pencil in different positions. Try this with all of your pencils to get an idea of the variety of textures that can be achieved by simply changing the direction and grip of the pencil.

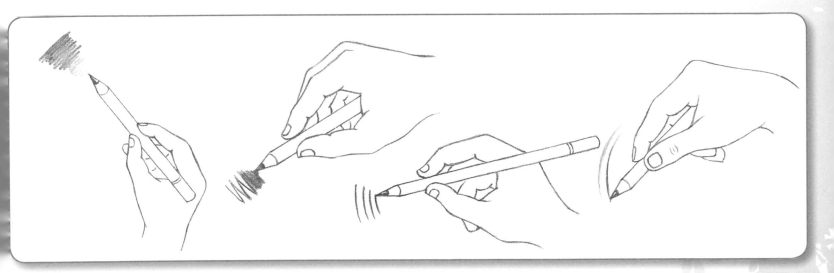

Feathers: Use an HB or 2B pencil and very lightly, draw a sharp stroke, blurring toward the end. All strokes should be parallel to each other and at a slight angle.

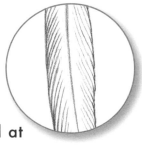

SCALES: Scales are a lot of fun to draw. Start with light criss-cross strokes. Add to these, detailed cross-hatches for dark areas. Small scales are individually shaded based on where the light is coming from. See page 10 for details.

FUR: Fur is soft but not as smooth as feathers. Use light parallel strokes in the direction of the body of the animal.

Shiny Skin: Shading for skin is smooth where you can't see the pencil strokes. The most important part of drawing shiny skin is adding the highlights.

Red-Eyed Tree Frog

The Red-Eyed Tree Frog (*Agalychnis callidryas***) has bold, bright red eyes. Its body is neon green splashed with blue or yellow, with bright blue upper legs and orange or red feet. This frog can change its color with its mood from a darker green to a reddish-brown. The males are about 2 in. (5 cm) in length, and the females about 3 in. (7.6 cm).**

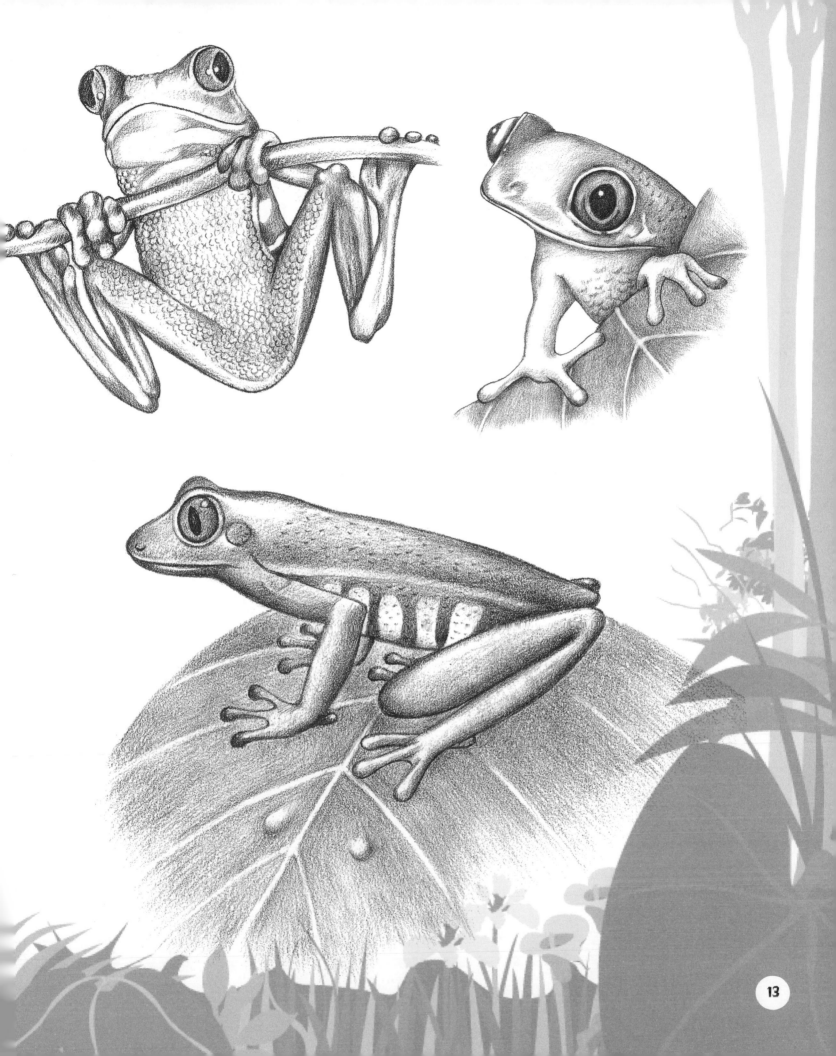

• HOW TO DRAW RAINFOREST ANIMALS

14

Step 1

Start by drawing an oval for the head and the spine of the sitting frog.

Step 2

In the head oval, add a circle for the eye. Add another semi-circle behind the first oval for the frog's second eye. One horizontal line in the head oval will create the frog's mouth. Add the basic skeleton for the legs and feet with lines for the limbs and circles for the digits.

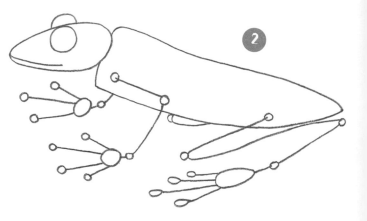

Step 3

Now connect the head oval with the shape made for the body. Add an ellips- inside the eye oval for the frog's pupil. underneath the line for the mouth, draw a small line connecting the lower part of the face to the main body. Cover the joints and bones with cylinders of vario shapes, giving volume to the frog's limb

Step 4

Erase the extra guidelines. Draw a small circle for the nostril near the front of the head oval. Add a curve on the top of the eye circle to add a touch of protrusion. Draw a reverse C for the frog's ear. Add the bars on its belly. Connect the shoulder and the lower limb with a line and encase the belly bars inside. The frog is ready for shading and highlighting.

Step 5

Now start shading and highlighting. See page 10 for details.

DID YOU KNOW?

This frog's name, *callidryas*, comes from the Greek *kallos*, meaning beautiful, and *dryas*, meaning tree sprite.

Details

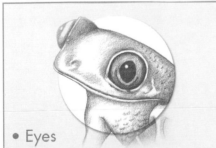

• Skin

• Eyes

The eyes of this frog protrude. This means they bulge out of the head. Draw small balls stuck on top of the head. There are two outer lines that represent the skin around the eyeball. Shade in-between the lines to show depth. Shade the inner pupil and highlight where the light hits it. Also, add more shading to the lower portion of the pupil for a three-dimensional effect.

This frog's skin is smooth and shiny. Don't show pencil strokes when shading and highlighting. Hold your pencil so you can cover the entire area in soft tones. Check out page 10 if you need a refresher on shading and highlighting.

Poison Dart Frog

There are four main groups of poison dart frogs: *Dendrobates*, *Epipedobates*, *Minyobates*, **and** *Phyllobates*. **These frogs can be red, blue, green, or yellow. They also have a variety of color patterns, from spots to stripes. There are 170 species of poison dart frogs, and most wear a bright splash of color.**

1

Step 1

Start by drawing an oval for the head and a spine running from it for the body.

2

Step 2

Add a guideline on the oval to show the direction in which the frog is facing. Draw horizontal lines for the eyes and the nose. Draw a big oval around the spine for the frog's body.

Step 3

Draw a large oval for the eye on the side facing you in the head oval and behind it, another half-oval for the other eye. Now add the basic skeleton for the legs and the feet with lines for the limbs and ovals for the digits.

3

Step 4

Erase the guidelines, and add cylinders for the frog's legs and feet. Add a tiny circle touching the top inside of the frog's eye for a highlight. Add a wavy curve on top of the torso oval. This will give the frog a three-dimensional feel and add volume to its body.

4

Step 5

Draw dots all over the body. Fill in the eye with a dark tone, leaving some areas white for highlights. Mark the areas on the body, such as the top of the head, the area around the eye, the underside of the legs, and the belly for shading in lighter tones.

Step 6

Now shade the entire body. The frog's skin is slimy, so it's a little shiny as well as bumpy on the back and neck. Start shading in light, circular rotations with a light pencil. Leave some gaps between the strokes for the lighter parts. Add another round of mid-tone on the light ones but don't cover the light tone entirely. Lastly, add darker tones to the areas around the edge of the mouth, on the protrusion of the eyes, on the upper arm and the forearm, and the hind legs. To give the effect of the slightly bumpy skin, hold the pencil's tip diagonally and apply some pressure to create a dark spot. Press it in for the mid-tones on the body. Add some color using your colored pencils.

DID YOU KNOW?

The poison dart frog has enough poison to kill about 2,000 people!

19

Emerald Tree Boa

The Emerald Tree Boa (*Corallus caninus*) is green and white in color and grows to be about 7¼ feet (2.2 m) long. It lives in trees, swamps, and marshes in rainforests. This snake specializes in hunting birds that perch near it. Its colors give it the appearance of a group of leaves stained with bird droppings!

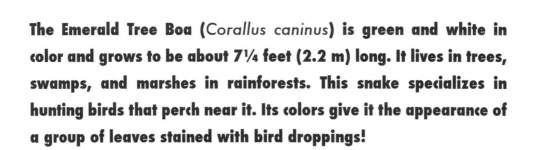

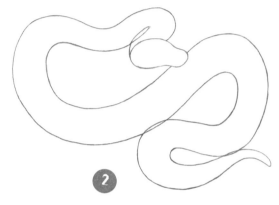

Step 1

Start by drawing two ovals in the proportions and positions shown. Add a long, curving line for the spine, starting from the head. These will be the head and the basic axis along which to draw the snake.

Step 2

Draw a shape that encloses the two ovals from the outside to give you the snake's head and snout. For its body, draw two parallel lines running along the right and left of the spine, tapering toward the tail.

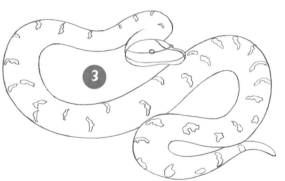

Step 3

Lightly draw lines across the head for the placement of the eyes and mouth.
For the scales, draw long, abstract shapes throughout the body except on the head. Vary these shapes and their positions as you move along.

Step 4

Now lightly draw cross-hatch lines throughout the body. These lines should not be straight so as to add dimension to the snake's body. Add circular eyes and a jagged mouth-line where indicated. Draw tiny C curves close together for the scales on the head and bigger ones around the mouth. Add a vertical line to the eye circle for the snake's pupil.

Step 5

It's time for the final effects! Leave the scales white and use a 2B pencil (technical) to darken the cross-hatch lines and a graphite HB pencil to lightly shade along the middle of the snake's body. These impressions will complete the three-dimensional effect. Don't forget to color!

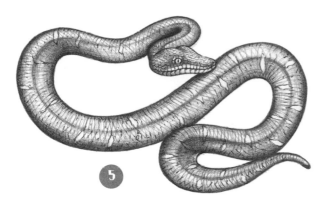

5

DID YOU KNOW?

The boa's top and bottom jaws are attached to each other with stretchy ligaments, enabling it to swallow animals wider than itself!

Details

• **Scales**

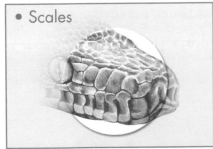

The emerald boa's most noticeable feature is its green color and irregular markings. When rendering the scales, darken the inside and leave the edges white. For the pattern, leave a few scales white. The scales on the boa follow a simple criss-cross pattern. Draw parallel lines in one direction and then the other to get a checkered pattern. Keep in mind the direction of the lines that follow the pipe-like body of the snake. This can really make your snake look three-dimensional.

• **Eyes**

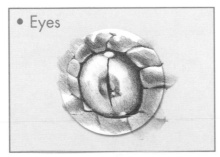

The eye of the boa is a single circle. Decide on the source of light and add a precise dark shadow in the opposite direction. Also look at the specific pattern on the eyeball and draw it according to the surface.

• **Cross-hatching**

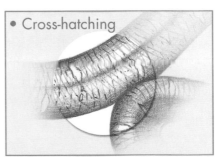

For cross-hatching, start with criss-cross strokes all over the body, keeping in mind the various contours. Start with darker strokes that slowly fade to white. First apply more pressure on a 4B or a 6B pencil to get a darker tone. Reduce it slowly to end in white space to bring out the highlights.

Jaguar

The Jaguar (*Panthera onca*) is the largest cat found in the rainforest and deserts of Central and South America. Fully-grown jaguars can vary from 5 to 9 feet (1.5 to 2.7 m) in length and can weigh up to 350 pounds (132 kg)! With its head and shoulders and short, muscular legs, the jaguar is a symbol of power, strength, and beauty.

Step 1

Start by drawing a circle for the jaguar's head. Then, draw a gently curving line that runs from the head along the spine to the tail.

Step 2

Lightly draw a vertical line for the placement of the nose and mouth and then a horizontal line for the placement of the eyes. Add two semi-circles at the top of the head for the ears. Now, draw an oval shape to form the front side of the body and a line to connect the back and neck.

Step 3

Draw the bones and joints, starting with the scapula (forms the shoulder) and the pelvis (forms the hips). The scapula connects to the bones of the front legs, and the pelvis connects to the back legs. Draw lines for the legs and small circles for the joints.

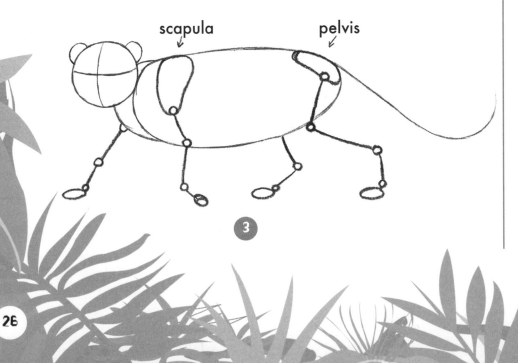

scapula   pelvis

Step 4

Draw two ovals for the eyes along the horizontal line you drew on the head. Add the lower jaw at the base of the circle. Draw a triangle for the nose along the vertical line, halfway between the eyes and the mouth. Draw tubes for the legs and tail.

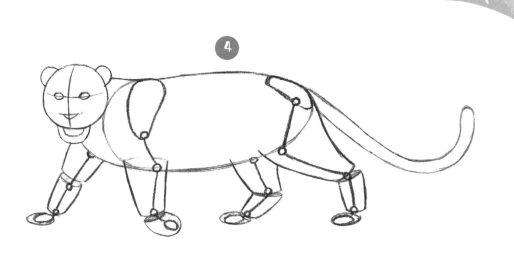

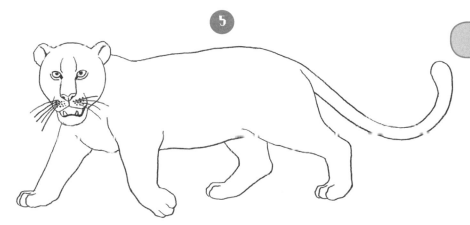

Step 5

It's time to fine-tune the lines! Erase the guidelines that you drew to define the outline of the jaguar. Join the outer lines of the tube shapes to form the legs.

The belly overlaps the lines of the legs farther away from you. Now, add the details to the eyes and nose. Make dotted lines above the mouth where the whiskers go. Add lines to the paws to form the toes.

Step 6

The most distinguishing characteristic of the jaguar is its coat, which is covered with marks called rosettes.

When drawing the rosettes, remember to vary the size and shape to break up the pattern and make it look more realistic. Don't make the shapes symmetrical.

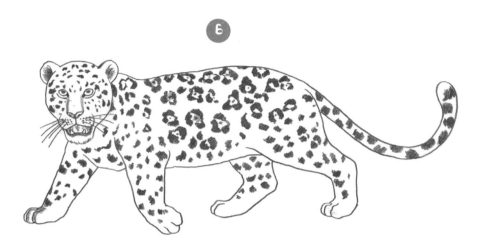

E

DID YOU KNOW?

Jaguars are the third largest cats. Only lions and tigers are bigger!

Step 7

Draw the whiskers from the dotted lines above the mouth. The rosettes are part of the fur, so fill them in by using uneven lines. Next, take an HB pencil and connect the rosettes by making light cross-hatch lines across the body. This will add some shading and make the rosettes look like part of the body. Use your pencil to create the highlights (light areas) and some shading (dark areas). Use the colored pencils to finish your drawing.

Details

• Eyes

First get the proper shape of the eyes. Then darken the outlines toward the corners of the eye. Be careful to maintain one source of light (light in just one direction). Draw the jaguar's eyes in a slanting position to give it a more menacing look. Shape another bigger circle around the eye, but in a lighter tone. All members of the cat family have a band of white underneath their eyes.

• Rosettes

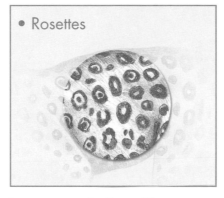

Rosettes are the flower-like patterns on the jaguar's body. First, look at the contours of the patterns and repeat them all over the body. Fill in the rosettes with a dark shade. Since they are part of the fur, render them in a scratch manner rather than filling them in neatly.

• Ears

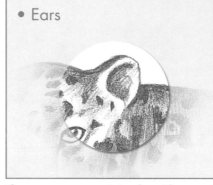

The ears are semi-circular. The most important thing is to get the placement of the ears in proportion to the head. Wait to do the details until you get the position right. Use a darker pencil for making the outlines bold, and some light pencil strokes for the hair in the ear. Then darken the inside of the ear to show depth.

Iguana

An iguana is a large lizard with a spiny crest along its back. Full-grown iguanas are usually between 4 and 7 feet (1.2 and 2m) in length including the tail, which makes up about half of the body length. Iguanas have long toes and claws to help them climb and grasp. Males have a flap of skin under their jaw called the dewlap that they raise to appear bigger than they really are, either to intimidate predators or impress females.

Step 1

Start by drawing an oval for the head and a vertical line for the iguana's position.

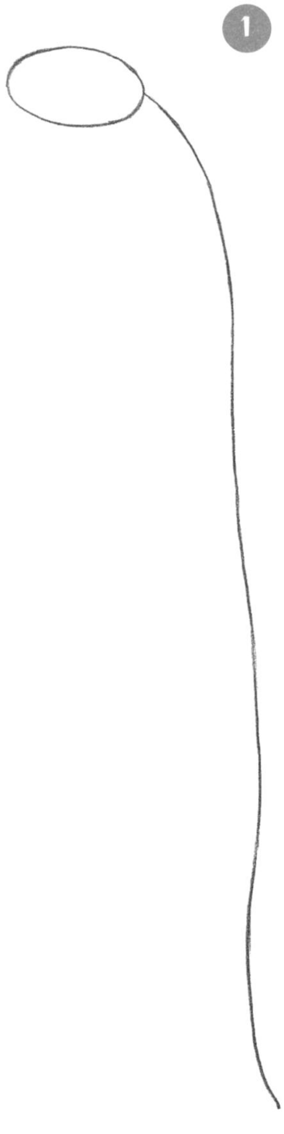

1

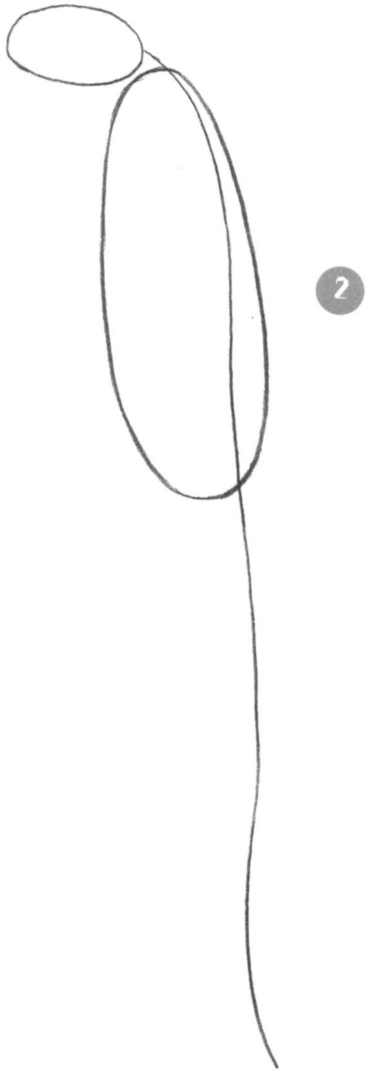

2

Step 2

Add an elongated oval along the top half of the vertical line for the iguana's torso.

Step 3

In the head oval, add horizontal guidelines for the eyes and mouth. Next, join the head and torso ovals. Follow this by adding lines and ovals for the front feet and legs. Draw fairly big ovals for the lizard's front feet. Draw the tail from the base of the torso to the tip of the spine.

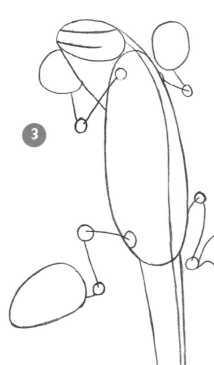

3

4

Step 4

Add an eye on the first horizontal guideline. Erase half of the inside part of the head oval and the top of the ellipse of the torso. Add cylinders on top of the joints and bones to give volume. Draw the iguana's claws on the inside of the feet ovals.

Step 5

Erase the guidelines. Now add an arc on the head for the crest. Join the cylinders of the feet and legs. Add the background of the tree.

5

Details

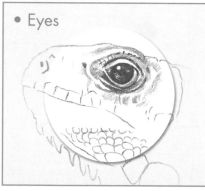

• Eyes

Before starting detailed shading, it's important to get the correct position and proportion of the iguana's eyes to the body. The spherical eye is covered with thin eyelids that don't have scales, so the shading there is smooth. The dark pupil covers most of the eye. In addition to the stark highlight, you can also add a sub-highlight of a lower intensity to add life to the image.

• Crest

The crest is a scaly growth of spikes that starts from the top of the head and runs the length of the iguana. Shade the smaller spikes as one form, but shade the bigger scales individually. Remember to draw the spikes at random to make them appear more realistic. The sharp spikes can be shaded with a defined outline using a pointed HB or 2B pencil.

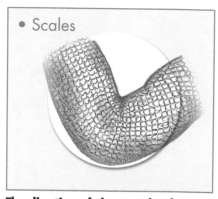

• Scales

The direction of the cross-hatches will follow the structure of the body part. Because the scales are on the skin, the shade on the body will not change. In places where they are more visible, add a lighter tone to show the light on every individual scale. Notice the different types of scales on the head, hand, mouth, and crest.

Step 6

For the detailing, draw long spikes in the arc for the crest. Then starting from the crest, draw short, thick spikes down to the tail. For the scales on the body, first draw arcs from one side of the body to the other, then overlap with diagonal arcs.

Step 7

Shade to finish. Add fishlike scales on the iguana's face. The scales around the mouth are bigger. Use a mid-tone pencil for the scales of the body, feet, legs, and tail. Don't forget to add some color!

DID YOU KNOW?

Green iguanas are so hardy that they can fall 40-50 feet to the ground without getting hurt!

Sugar Glider

The Sugar Glider (*Petaurus breviceps*) is a mammal found in Indonesia, New Guinea, New Zealand, and Australia. It's silver-gray in color and has a black stripe that runs down its body from nose to tail. It also has a dark stripe that runs from the outside corner of each eye to its ears. An adult sugar glider is about 5 to 7 inches (13 to 8 cm) long and weighs 3 to 4 ounces (85 to 133 g). Its tail is fluffy and is usually longer than its body.

1

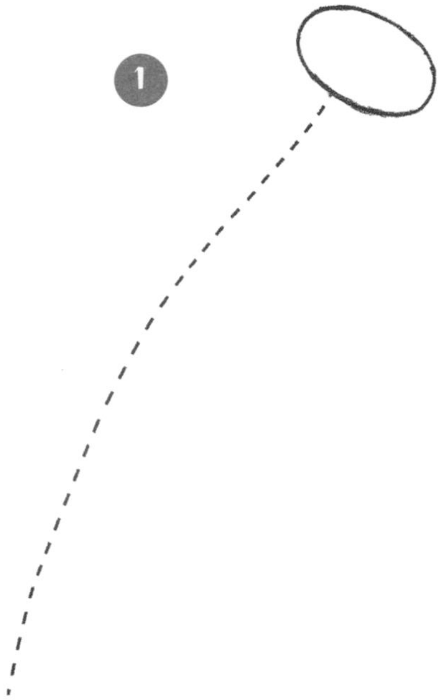

Step 1

Start by drawing an oval for the head and a dotted, slightly curving line for the spine that runs from the head and to the tip of the tail.

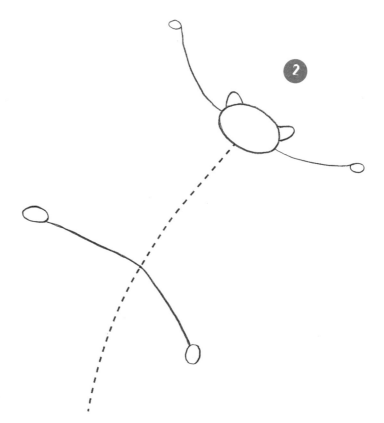

2

Step 2

Add two small semi-circles on top of the head for the ears. Add two small horizontal arcs on either side of the head oval. Also add two slightly curved arcs toward the lower end of the spine. These are for the legs of the sugar glider. Draw tiny ovals at the end of these lines for the paws.

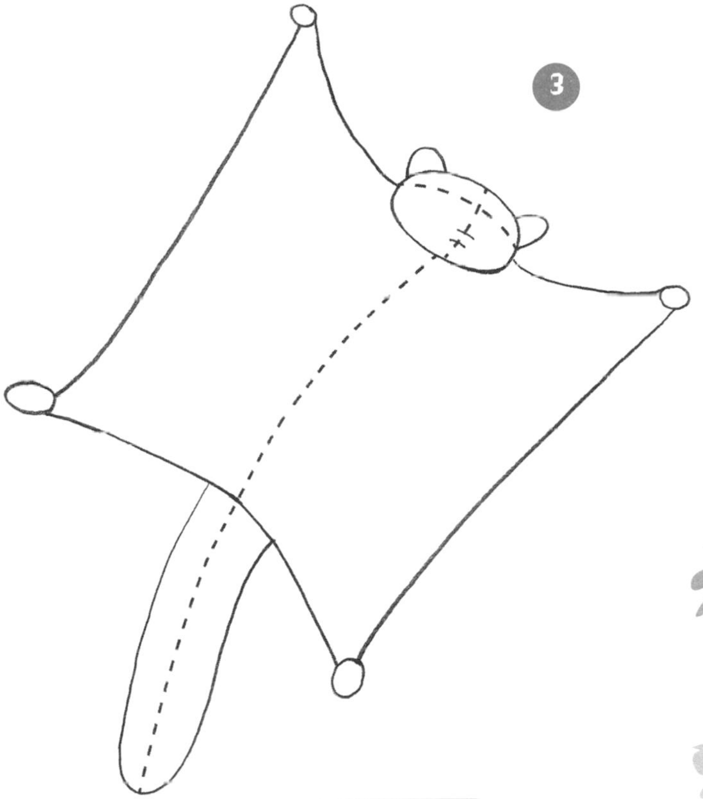

Step 3

Add guidelines on the head for the placement of the eyes, nose, and mouth. Connect the small feet paw ovals with vertical lines on either side of the spine. Then draw a thick tail around the remaining portion of the spine.

3

4

Step 4

Draw two circles for the eyes of the sugar glider, two tiny dots for the nose, and a small horizontal line for the mouth. Now erase the spine and add an oval in the middle for the belly of the sugar glider. Also erase the line cutting across the tail.

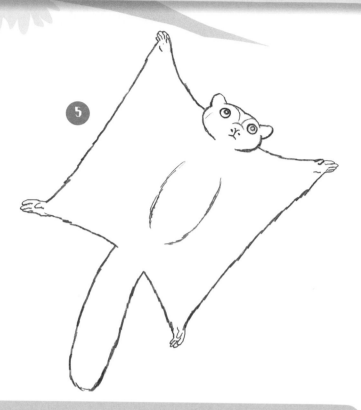

Step 5

Add two small circles within the eyes for the highlights. Draw two lines in the middle of the head that come together at the bridge of the nose. Detail the digits on the paws. Give the outlines an uneven effect for the fur.

Details

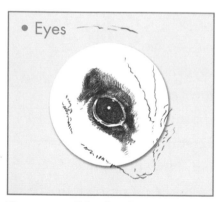

• Eyes

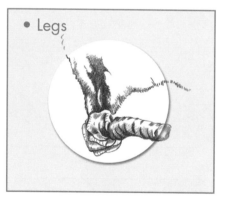

• Legs

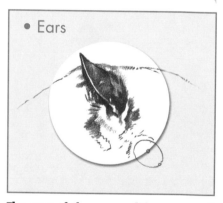

• Ears

The sugar glider has big, dark eyes. Its eyelids are thin skin folds that are lighter than the eyes. The fur gets darker as you near the eyes, so you need to carefully plan the direction of the pencil strokes around the eyes. Shade the eye in a dark tone, and leave some highlights for that shine in the eye!

The limbs of the sugar glider are tiny paws at the end of the wings. The fingers are bony with sharp nails. The bones are visible as the fingers curl over the object. Leave a lighter area on top and darken the gaps between the fingers. Add a couple of hard pencil strokes to show the rough skin texture on the fingers.

The ears of the sugar glider are small and triangular. The hair on the ear is smaller compared to that of the rest of the body, so use small, fine pencil strokes on the skin of the ears. Also notice the direction of the hair where the ear starts.

6

Step 6

Fill in the area outside the inner circles in the eyes and the V pattern on the forehead. Add small whiskers around the nose. Add scratch lines all along the body, leaving a small space next to the outlines. Take a blunt HB pencil and shade the fur in the middle of the body.

Step 7

For the finishing touches, add shading around the eyes in a tone lighter than that of the eye. You can add some darker strokes in between to suggest depth. Be sure to use your colored pencils, too.

7

DiD YOU KNOW?

Sugar gliders can glide great distances through the air, sometimes covering as much distance as that of a football field!

Macaw

A macaw is the largest and showiest member of the parrot family. It has a slender body, long wings, a long tapered tail, and an oversized head and beak. The Hyacinth macaw is the largest — about 40 inches (100 cm) in length with a wingspan of nearly 4 feet (1.2 m), while the noble macaw is the smallest — about 13 inches (33 cm) in length with a 7- to 7½ - inch (18- to 19-cm) wingspan. Common colors of macaws are blue, blue and gold, green, green and red, and red and yellow.

Step 1

Start by drawing four vertical ovals in descending sizes for the body of the macaw. Draw two horizontal ovals for the head and beak.

Step 2

Connect the head oval with that of the body from the outside. Also add two semi-ovals on either side of the first body oval for the wings.

Step 3

Lightly draw a guideline along the head for the placement of the eye. Add a line across the smaller oval to distinguish the upper and lower part of the beak. In the body oval, add two circles for the macaw's phalanges (toe bones). Erase the intersecting section of the tail oval in the body oval.

Step 4

Add the background of a tree and a branch for the bird to perch. Draw the branch running through its claws.

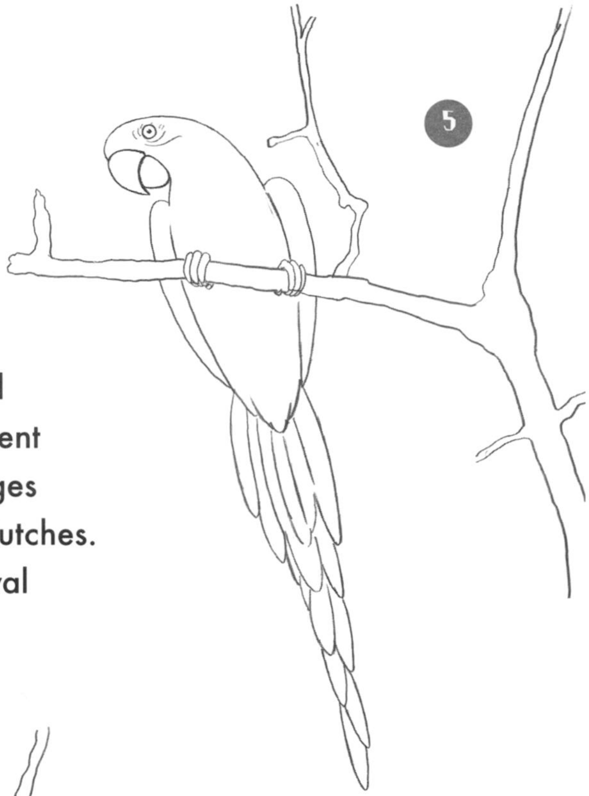

Step 5

Add details like lines under and around the bird's eye to represent tiny feathers. Draw the phalanges inside the ovals for the bird's clutches. Add long feathers within the oval guidelines for the tail.

Step 6

Shade the head and the body to give the effect of tightly packed, small feathers. Draw slanting lines along the spines of the feathers for detailing.

Step 7

Add shading and tones throughout the entire body and tail. Remember to go from light to dark. Give your macaw some color, too.

DiD you Know?

There are 17 living macaw species, along with a number of macaw hybrids.

Details

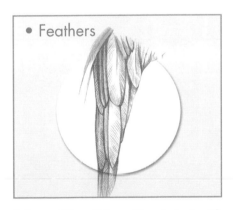

• Feathers

Take an HB or 2B pencil and start with a sharp stroke, blurring toward the end. The strokes should be parallel.

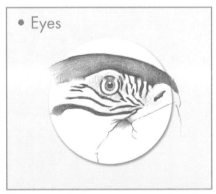

• Eyes

The eyes of the macaw are tiny, but the circles around the pupil make it seem wide-eyed. Draw two circles around the pupils and darken the inner circle, leaving some white for the highlight. Also detail the small feathers around the eyes.

• Beak

A macaw has a huge beak, curved inward with a slight bulge. The smoothness of the beak can be shaded with a 2B or 4B pencil. To define the subtle curve, add an extra dark tone near the top of the beak.

Spider Monkey

The Spider Monkey (*Ateles geoffroyi geoffroyi*) is characterized by long, slender limbs and great agility. Its tail is longer than its body and is used as an extra hand. This monkey leaps through trees, sprawling out like a spider with one arm-stride covering up to 40 feet (12.2 m). Its body is about 2 feet (.6 m) long and the tail up to 3 feet (.9 cm) long, and it weighs around 13 to 17 pounds (5.9 to 7.7 kg).

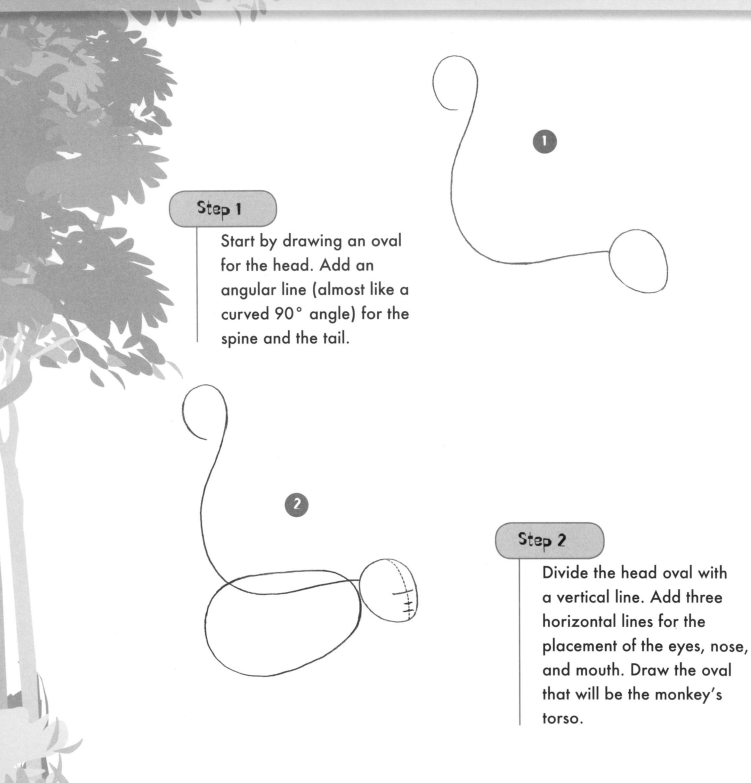

Step 1

Start by drawing an oval for the head. Add an angular line (almost like a curved 90° angle) for the spine and the tail.

Step 2

Divide the head oval with a vertical line. Add three horizontal lines for the placement of the eyes, nose, and mouth. Draw the oval that will be the monkey's torso.

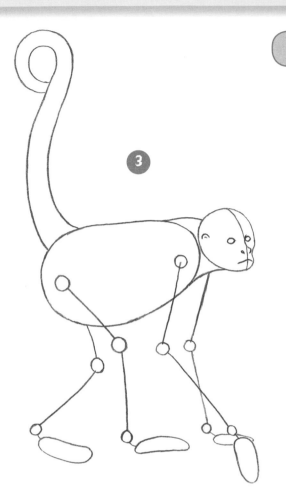

Step 3

Draw two small circles on either side of the vertical line for the eyes. Connect the head and the torso. Add small circles for the joints and lines for the bones of the hands and legs. Add volume to the tail.

Step 4

Now add two big circles around the small eye circles. Shape up the nose and add the upper part of the monkey's ear. Add cylinders for the arms, hands, and legs. Draw fingers in the hand and feet ellipses.

Step 5

Add the background of rocks for the monkey to walk on. Along the guidelines of the two circles around the eyes, make an outcrop of hair. Do the same along the ear down through the ridge of the jaw and up to the chin. Erase the guidelines and add an edgy finish to the entire outline.

Details

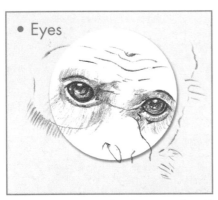

• Eyes

The highlights in both eyes should be according to a single light source. The outline of the pupil (the outer part of the eye) is darker than the iris (the middle part of the eye).

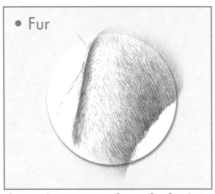

• Fur

The easiest way to draw the fur is to decide on the light and shade areas on the body. Give the fur a middle tone as a base, then add darker pencil strokes for the fine hair. Keep the strokes the same length and going in the same direction. Start with a hard stroke that gently fades out. Don't close the outlines of the body in a single line; instead, keep the edges rugged to get a hairy appearance.

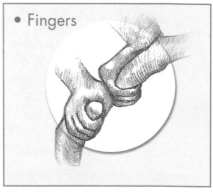

• Fingers

The spider monkey's hands are similar to human hands, with a thumb on one side and fingers on the other. Draw a square for the palm and mark the position of the fingers according to the action of the hand. Then detail the fingers.

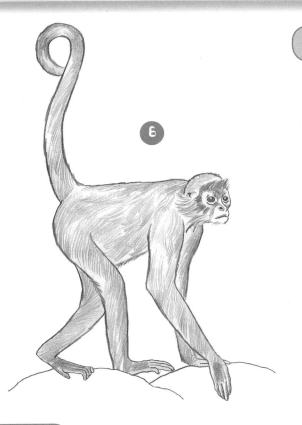

Step 6

For the hair, draw wavy lines on the entire body. Don't cross-hatch the lines. Keep leaving space between strokes for the light falling on the hair. Make the eyes dark, leaving space for highlights. Add two lines, one above and one below the eyes. The skin on the temples, cheeks, and nose of the monkey is darker.

Step 7

Add dark tones on the outcrop of hair on the forehead and around the eyes. Also darken the hair on the forearms, hind legs, knees, and feet. When drawing hair, repeat the strokes going in the same direction as the previous strokes. Now add a bit of color.

DiD YOU KNOW?

Relative to its size, the spider monkey has a larger brain than most other monkeys.

Okapi

The Okapi (*Okapia johnstoni*) is the only known living relative of the giraffe and is found in the tropical forests of the Republic of Congo (formerly Zaire). It is reddish-brown in color and has zebra-like stripes on its hindquarters and upper legs. It has a long neck and large and flexible ears. It is about 5 feet (1.5 m) tall at the shoulders and weighs about 450 to 550 pounds (200 to 250 kg).

• HOW TO DRAW RAINFOREST ANIMALS

Start by drawing a triangle with rounded corners for the head of the okapi. Beginning at the head, draw a slanting line that gently dips straight down. This makes the basic guidelines for the neck, back, and back leg of the okapi.

1

Draw the basic shapes for the neck, belly, legs, and hooves of the okapi. Draw a tiny circle slightly off-center, toward the top of the triangle for the eye. Draw guidelines for the ears.

2

Connect all the body shapes from the outside to create the torso and legs. Add the nose and mouth detail in the form of a small semi-circle and a small dash. Add two overlapping ovals on the top of the head for the ears.

3

(4)

Step 4

Add two small horns at the top of the head. Erase all the lines of the shapes within the body.

(5)

Step 5

The most distinguishing feature of the okapi is its striped legs. Detail these patterns as shown.

(6)

Step 6

To complete the image, start shading with small pencil strokes — light ones first, followed by darker tones. Carefully leave the stripes on the legs unshaded as they are nearly white. Add some color, if you wish.

DiD You Know?

At 14 inches (36 cm), the okapi's tongue is so long that it can lick its eyelids to clean them.

Golden Lion Tamarin

The Golden Lion Tamarin (*Leontopithecus rosalie*) prefers primary lowland tropical forests from sea level to 3300 feet (1000 m). Golden lion tamarins are omnivorous, feeding on fruits, gum, nectar, insects, and small vertebrates. They live mostly in trees and are active during the daytime. This animal is usually found at heights of 10 to 30 feet (3 to 10 m) above the forest floor. It sleeps there at night in tangled vegetation or, more often, in a hole in a tree, such as an abandoned woodpecker nest.

Step 1

Draw a circle for the head and a curved line that will form the spine and the tail.

1

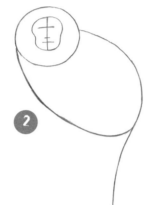

2

Step 2

Next, make a rough outline of the face. The first circle you drew will become the monkey's mane. Draw a big oval for the body with the remaining line as the tail. Within the shape drawn for the face, mark guidelines for the eyes, nose, and mouth as shown.

Step 3

On the face guidelines, draw two small circles for the eyes, two dots for the nose, and a horizontal line for the mouth. In the body oval, draw joints and bones of the monkey. Add ovals for the hands and feet. Give volume to the tail.

Draw a horizontal branch for the monkey to sit on.

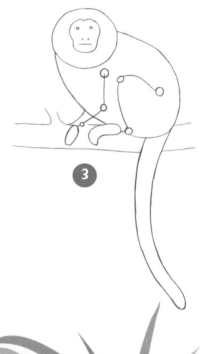

3

Step 4

Start adding details to the monkey's face. Around the shape of the face, start drawing the hair of the monkey's mane. Draw cylinders for the arms and legs, and draw fingers within the hands and feet ovals. Since the monkey is squatting, make its thigh an oval shape. Add an off-shoot to the main branch with some leaves on it.

4

Step 5

Work on the monkey's fur, curving the lines as shown. Use a uniform light tone throughout the body. Try to avoid a cross-hatch.

5

Step 6

Now begin the final shading. Press your pencil hard to get dark tones of hair where needed, especially in the mane, at the elbows, and along the spine. Finally shade in the leaves and branches, and add some color.

6

DID YOU KNOW?

When threatened, the tamarin raises its mane and fluffs up its fur to give it the appearance of being bigger than it really is.